THE VISIONARY LIGHTS FROM A DARK MIND

Sneha Jain

Printed and bound in India

Title: The Visionary Lights From A Dark Mind
Language: English
Character set encoding: UTF-8

First published by

An Imprint of Blue Rose Publishers

Head Office: 123, First Floor,
Ansal Bhawan, 16, K.G. Marg,
Connaught Place, New Delhi - 110001
+91-8882 898 898

Wordsbrew
An imprint of BlueRose Publishers

DEDICATED

TO THE ***READER***:-

*"**MAY YOU FIND HAPPINESS ,IN THIS NOT SO HAPPY WORLD.**"*

ACKNOWLEDGEMENTS

The world is a better place, thanks to people who want to develop and lead others. What makes it even better are people who share the gift of their time to mentor future leaders. Thank you to everyone who strives to grow and help others grow.

I am eternally thankful to God, my Parents and My Teachers who have supported me and given me the potential to write and think creatively.

I am also heartily thankful to each individual in the publications ,for helping me in the smooth and wonderful publishing of my book.

*-**Sneha Jain***

FOREWORD

I was eighteen , when I realized that my interest and passion lies in writing. Probably, that year, on one of the days, during the months of October and November, as my twelfth grade board exams were nearing, my anxiety level was also was going through the roof. It was that moment , when I decided to introspect myself, as to what I am capable of in my near future .That self-introspection session made me realize my own potential.

And as I joined the college, I still was not able to gather enough confidence to write and put my thoughts on paper. But ,the various competitions, the teachers ,the authorities motivated me to pursue my passion.

I always write my thoughts or poems in my diary or a notebook, but now, it is my first attempt to combine all my poems in a book and get it published.

I thank my parents, college authorities ,teachers to motivate me and encourage me .

August 05,2020
SNEHA JAIN

PREFACE

ABOUT THE AUTHOR :- *Sneha Jain grew up in Karnal, Haryana ,India. She is an undergraduate in B.A English Honors. She is an inquisitive person since her infancy. Creativity ,in all aspects has been her power. This is her first time seeking representation for an anthology or a collection of her poems.*

ABOUT THE BOOK:- *"THE VISIONARY LIGHTS FROM A DARK MIND" is an anthology by Sneha Jain, it contains different types and kinds of easily relatable and readable poetries, all about the real world with a hint of imagination.*

CONTENTS

1. A BUBBLY GIRL

A happy ,bubbly girl,
As beautiful as a pearl.
Although, she was full of flaws,
But, never deprived of applause.

Soft spoken by heart,
Ego! nah.. quite apart.
To her, respecting elders was obligatory,
No statement about her was defamatory.

A happy , bubbly girl,
As beautiful as a pearl.

2. A CANNINE!

At midnight,
Frightened to walk alone ,
Because they may bite!
One drooling for bone,
Another for body,
Nearby she sees nobody.
Meanwhile, one of them growled,
The other jumped and howled.
Now, she is adamant to believe
A canine, unlike humans, is protective.

3. A MOMENT

Winds blowing and birds chirping,

Flowers blooming and leaves rustling.

A wonderful morning,

To cheer her at moment.

A moment for herself.

Now, it's just her and her cup of tea,

As she works whole day like a busy bee.

This weather, this moment

Is what she captures in her mind and heart forever,

This one moment made her feel lively and beautiful like never ever.

4. A SPELL OF GOOD WEATHER

The radiant sun,

The breeze, cool and sudden.

Beautiful and lofty palm trees.

Desire for time to freeze.

5. AN INTROVERT

I sat there enervated,

Wondering why were we even invited!

The people around me are supposedly, choking me,

After all , these gatherings are not my cup of tea!

Oh! how I miss my room,

The crowds, for me , are no less than a doom.

6. BROTHER

The soft hearted brother,
Splendid dark haired youngster.
Our creative photographer,
Melophile , to him we consider.
An epicure yet so willowy,
Sober antiquated and elementary.

7. DARKNESS

The only darkness one should adore,
That too by the sea shore.
Dark water, Dark sky,
That too in the month of July!

Oh! A feast for the eyes and soul,
The icy cold waves of wind,
The silent and peaceful stroll,
Refreshes the mind.

A wide hearty smile,
After a long while.
The only darkness one should adore,
That too by the sea shore.

8. DEVOID OF IDENTITY

"Petite, beefy or podgy" ,

These comments made her uneasy.

Not a cent of self love left,

She felt bereft.

9. EQUALITY

Male, Female or Other,
Why at all, shall we bother!
Now that we support females, a few,
Need to support transgenders too?
Maybe, law favors them,
To this law, our mentality shall condemn.
We strongly abide by myths,
Neither law nor pride marches, to us, can convince.

10. FAMILY

The world is chaotic,

The life is hectic.

The need of peace,

And the view of beautiful mountain trees.

The foggy weather,

And the family together.

11. FRIENDSHIP

The mutual affection,

An immortal connection.

The two girls,

Their laughter and twirls.

Adorable sunset,

Perfect silhouette.

Carefree souls,

"Bestfriends" , to them ,

The world calls.

12. GALE

The howling gales,
Deeper in sea, went, the whales.
It seemed as if trees doubled over,
Nowhere to take a cover.
The house doors, bolted,
The shops ,closed.
Could hardly trail.
Past the violent gale.

13. GLAMOUR

Alluring beauty,

Fragrance fruity.

Sparkling glamour,

Her immortal armor.

14. LIFE

So unpredictable and short,

Do not rely on "what if not?".

Moments, some as sweet as sugar,

Some as bitter as ginger.

Failure or pain,

Always try again.

The cycle of life never ends,

No matter however , whatever , whenever one tends.

15. OPEN YOUR EARS!

She is black,

But where does she lack?

She is fat,

But she loves her curves,

REMEMBER THAT!

She is short,

But she has her family support.

16. PAIN OR GAIN

A long way to go,
Does not matter, fast or slow.
Hard work and failure,
"Trying Again" is the only savior.
Giving up may be a choice,
But gains after pains , make a rejoicing noise.
The people are backbiting,
The friends are depreciating.
But , one day,
Success shall come your way.

17. POVERTY

The tatters barely covered their body,

Their surroundings were dirty.

Sylphlike creatures,

The sole of the foot , covered with ulcers.

Our leftovers,

Their life savers.

18. RAIN! RAIN! RAIN!

Under the perpetual glaring sun,

The rhythm of the rain and

her heartbeat battled,

As the lustrous rainbow dazzled.

19. SCENT

Through the floral scents,

Presence of her mother she apprehends.

The earthy fragrance,

Symbolizing the love in abundance.

20. SELF -HATRED

A fat, dark complexioned girl,
Each strand of her hair, an imperfect curl.
Heavy chest, heavy back,
"Bad appetite", her each snack.

Her intelligence and talents,
Covered by her flaws.
Supported by Parents,
but not by In- Laws.

Destined to be ugly, she thought,
But the truth was, she never fought.

21. SOLACE

I stood there , under murky clouds,
Just me, away from the crowds.
The breeze caressing me,
The feel, one can adore for eternity.
The pitter-patter sound,
The petrichor from the ground,
Oh! how comforting it was,
Well, just because!

22. THE BEAUTIES OF NATURE

The limpid grey eyes,

Admiring the grey rhenish skies.

The brisk keen mountain air,

This breathtaking picturesque view,

so rare.

23. THE EXECRABLE HER!

They see her blubber,
Judge her color.
They gossip about her personality,
Question her morality.
They criticize her figure,
Label her as a gold digger.

24. THE SUNRISE

Bright golden rays,
How peaceful the world stays!

The moment to adore,
Unable to ignore.
The beauty, the peace
May this moment never cease!

Bright golden rays,
How peaceful the world stays!

25. UNSAFE SOULS!

Out in the twilight,

Her body is the highlight.

Monsters drooling,

The lust ruling.

An infant or the old women,

Molested by the growling men.

Candle march or hunger strike,

Unfortunately, these assaults are still at spike.

www.ingramcontent.com/pod-product-compliance
Ingram Content Group UK Ltd.
Pitfield, Milton Keynes, MK11 3LW, UK
UKHW042000190726
13854UKWH00005B/2082